W9-BUB-360

3 1160 00523 6901

Bloomfield Twp. Public Library
1099 Lone Pine Road
Bloomfield Hills, MI 48302-2410

It's Catching

Head Lice

Angela Royston

Bloomfield Twp. Public Library
1099 Lone Pine Road
Bloomfield Hills, MI 48302-2410

© 2002 Reed Educational & Professional Publishing
Published by Heinemann Library,
an imprint of Reed Educational & Professional Publishing,
Chicago, Illinois
Customer Service 888-454-2279
Visit our website at www.heinemannlibrary.com

All rights reserved. No part of this publication may be reproduced or transmitted in any form or by any means, electronic or mechanical, including photocopying, recording, taping, or any information storage and retrieval system, without permission in writing from the publisher.

Designed by David Oakley/Arnos Design
Originated by Dot Gradations
Printed in Hong Kong, China

06 05 04 03 02
10 9 8 7 6 5 4 3 2

Library of Congress Cataloging-in-Publication Data
Royston, Angela.
     Head lice / Angela Royston.
        p. ; cm. -- (It's catching)
     Includes bibliographical references and index.
     ISBN 1-58810-229-7
     1. Pediculosis--Juvenile literature. [1. Lice.]
     [DNLM: 1. Lice Infestations--prevention & control--Juvenile
     Literature. 2. Pediculus--Juvenile Literature. WR 375 R892h 2001] I.
     Title. II. Series.

RL764.P4 R69 2001
616.5'7--dc21

                                        00-012834

Acknowledgments
The Publishers would like to thank the following for permission to reproduce photographs:
Bubbles: pp. 5 Ian West, 20, 25 Jennie Woodcock, 29 Pauline Cutler; Corbis: pp. 7 Carl Purcell, 26 Roger Ressmeyer; pp. 18, 19, 21 Gareth Boden; p. 22 Martin Soukias; p. 4 NHPA; p. 28 Zefa/Powerstock; p. 10 Robert Harding; p. 8 Sally and Richard Greenhill; Science Photo Library: pp. 6, 12 Mark Clarke, 14 Sinclair Stammers, 15 J. C. Revy, 17 David Scharf, 24 Dr. Chris Hale; p. 9 Jerome Tisne/Stone; Tony Stone: pp. 11 Bob Torrez, 16 Tim Flach, 23 Andy Sacks; pp. 13, 27 Trevor Clifford.

Cover photograph reproduced with permission of Science Photo Library.

Every effort has been made to contact copyright holders of any material reproduced in this book. Any omissions will be rectified in subsequent printings if notice is given to the Publisher.

Some words are shown in bold, **like this.** You can find out what they mean by looking in the glossary.

Contents

JUN 0 2 2003

What Are Head Lice?

Head lice are small **insects** that live in human hair. This louse has been **magnified** so that you can see what it looks like.

A louse is actually about as big as the head of a pin. It moves so fast through the hair that it can be very difficult to spot.

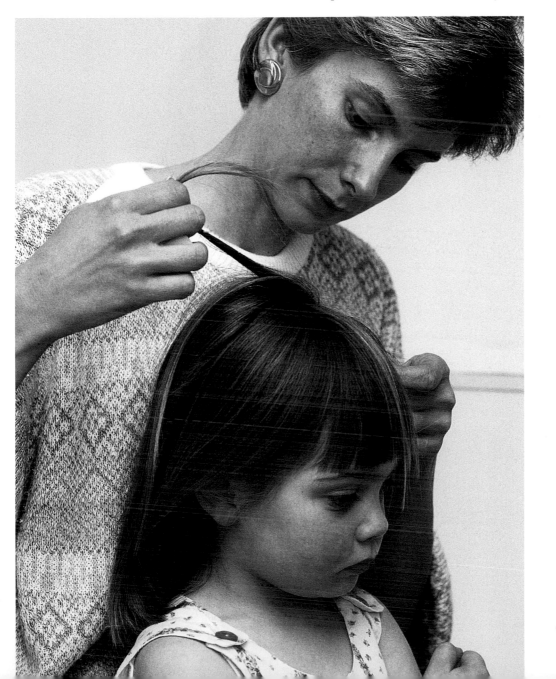

A Healthy Scalp

This is a **magnified** photo of a **scalp,** which is the layer of skin that covers your head. Hair grows longer and thicker on the scalp than anywhere else on the body.

Hair protects your scalp from the sun's rays. It also helps to keep you warm. It keeps the heat in your body from escaping through your scalp.

Passing Them On

Head lice pass very easily from one person to another. Your head often touches the heads of your friends and classmates. When two heads touch, lice can crawl from one head to the other.

Your hair also touches the heads of the other people in your family. If one person has head lice, soon all of his or her friends and family could have them, too!

Who Gets Head Lice?

Anyone who has hair can get head lice!
People with short hair can catch them
just as easily as people with long hair.

If you have head lice, it does not mean that your hair is dirty. Lice like a clean **scalp.** Young people are more likely to catch head lice because their heads touch each other more often.

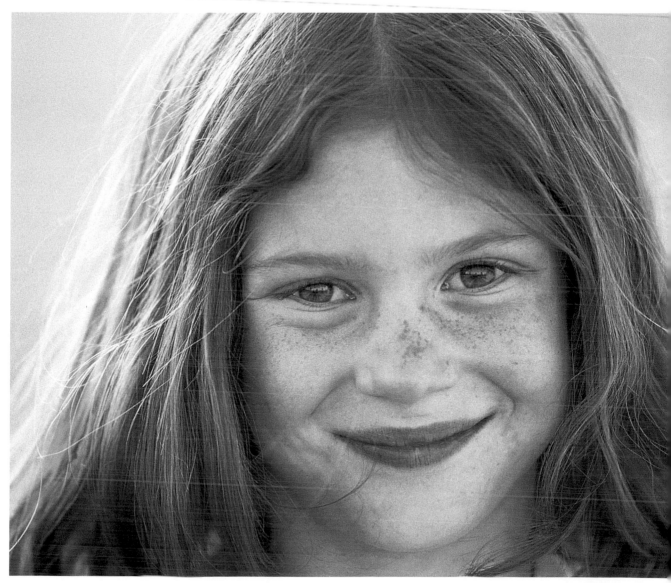

First Signs

The first thing a louse does when it crawls into your hair is bite your **scalp.** Some people begin to itch as soon as the louse bites them.

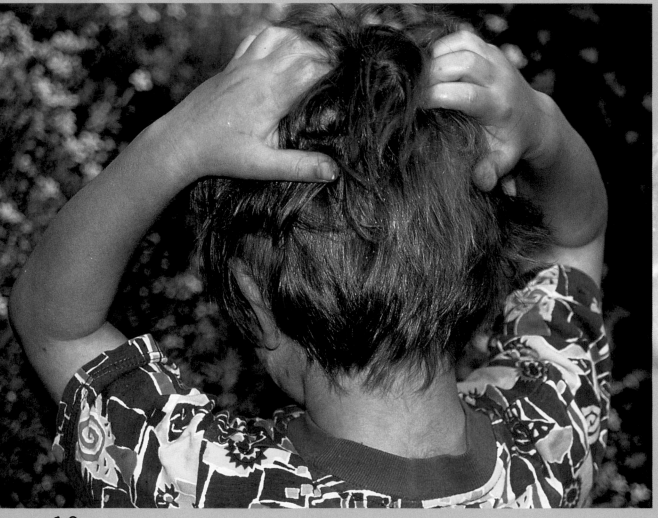

Other people do not itch until several weeks later. You cannot get rid of lice by washing your hair with ordinary **shampoo.**

What Happens Next

The louse lays many tiny eggs on the hair close to the **scalp.** The eggs stick to the hair so hard that you cannot get them out with a regular comb.

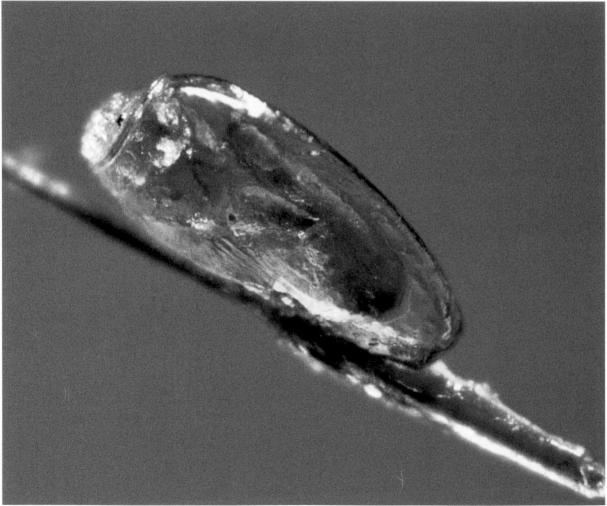

After about a week, a young louse **hatches** from the egg. The empty shell stays glued to the hair and is called a **nit.**

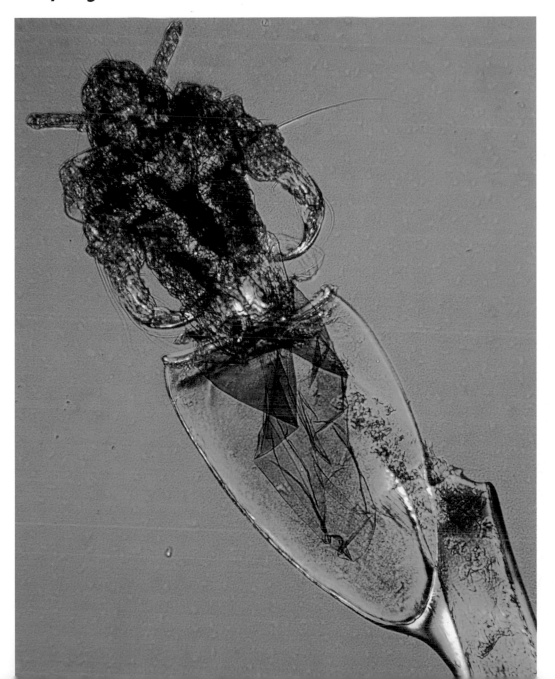

Many Lice

The young lice feed by sucking blood from the **scalp.** They have special claws that grip the hair.

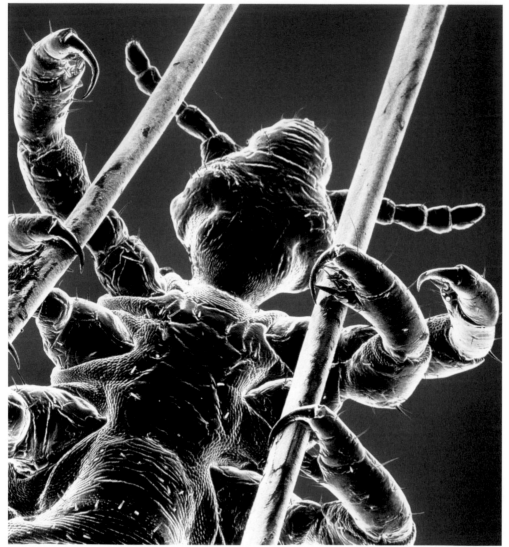

The young lice grow fast. They start to lay eggs themselves when they are only about ten days old. Soon the hair is full of lice!

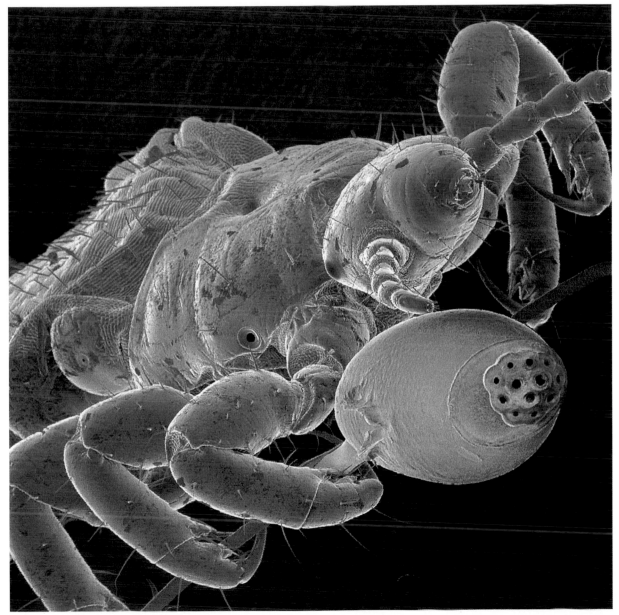

Getting Rid of Lice

Special **shampoos** contain strong **chemicals** that kill the lice. Sometimes, though, these shampoos do not work because the lice get used to them.

Some people use a special **herbal** shampoo to kill the lice instead. Everyone in the family has to wash their hair at the same time.

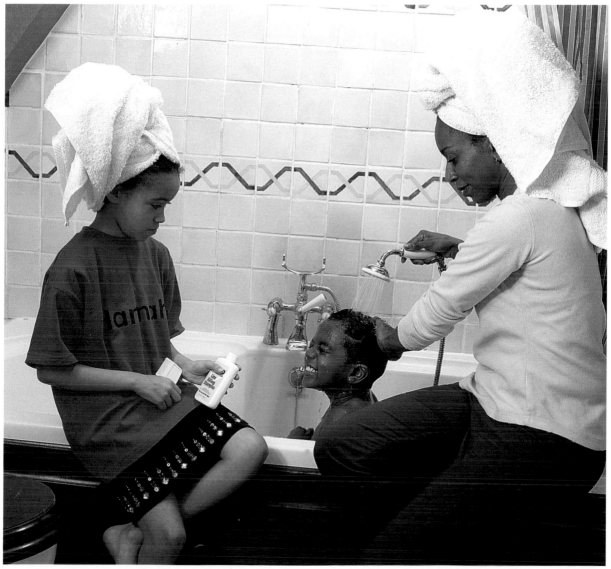

Combing Out the Lice

Nit combs have teeth that are very close together. Once you have used the special **shampoo,** you can use a nit comb to comb out the dead lice and nits.

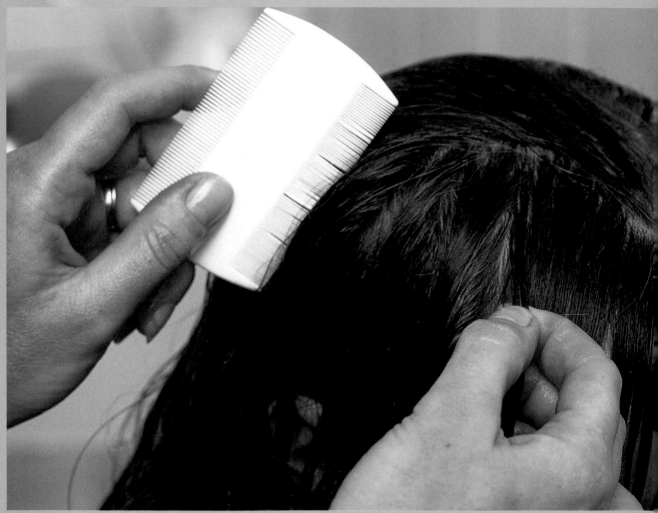

Another way to get rid of lice is to soak the hair in **olive oil** and leave it overnight. Then you can comb the lice out with a nit comb. If this doesn't work, you will have to use the special shampoo.

Bug-busting

Two weeks after **shampooing** or oiling your hair, you must do it again. This is to kill any lice that have **hatched** since then.

The best way to get rid of lice completely is for everyone in your class, or school, to shampoo their heads on the same night.

On the Lookout

The sooner you notice that you have lice, the sooner you can get rid of them. Check your hair regularly for **nits** like these.

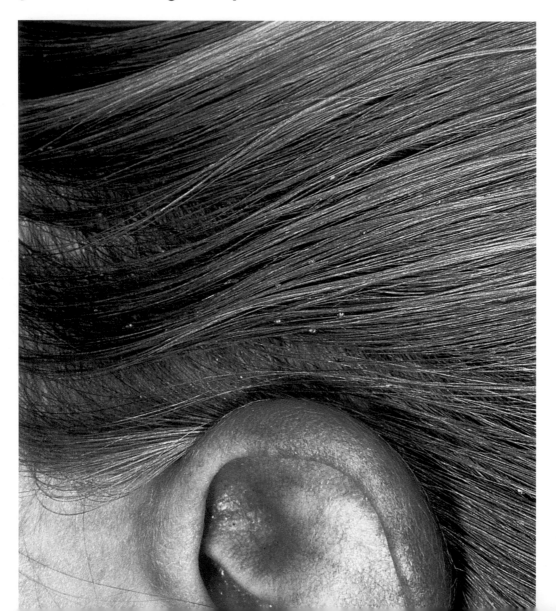

If your head itches, ask a parent to comb your hair using a nit comb. Then you can look for lice on the comb. You can even use the nit comb yourself, but tell your parents if you find anything.

Staying Healthy

You cannot stop lice from getting into your hair, and lice like clean hair just as much as you do. If you live a healthy life, though, you will get fewer other illnesses.

Eat good food and get lots of exercise.
Keep yourself clean, wash your hands often,
and make sure you get plenty of sleep.

Think About It!

Maria says that **braiding** her hair helps to stop her from getting head lice. Do you think that she is right or wrong?*

Sam's friends found out that he has head lice. They won't play with him because they say he is dirty. Are they right?*

*Read page 30 to find out.

Answers

Page 28

Lice will crawl into any hair they come into contact with, so Maria can still catch head lice. Hair pulled close to the head in **braids** or a ponytail may be less likely to touch another person's hair though.

Page 29

Having head lice does not mean that you are dirty. In fact, head lice prefer clean hair. Sam must have caught them from someone else who had them. His friends may already be infected, too. It is unkind not to play with him, and it will not stop them from getting head lice from someone else.

Stay Healthy and Safe!

1. Always tell an adult if you feel sick or think there is something wrong with you.

2. Never take any **medicine** or use any **ointment** unless it is given to you by an adult you trust.

3. Remember, the best way to stay healthy and safe is to eat good food, drink lots of water, keep clean, exercise, and get lots of sleep.

Glossary

braiding criss-crossing three strands of hair together to form a braid

chemical substance that something is made of

hatch when an animal breaks out of the egg in which it has formed

herbal made from plants

insect small creature that has six legs

magnified made bigger so that you can see it more clearly

medicine substance used to treat or prevent an illness

nit empty shell that a louse leaves behind when it has hatched

ointment oily cream that often contains medicine and is rubbed onto the skin

olive oil thick liquid made by squeezing the fruits of the olive tree

scalp skin that covers your head and from which your hair grows

shampoo special kind of liquid soap used to wash your hair; the process of using shampoo while washing your hair

31

Index

More Books to Read

Gordon, Melanie A. *Let's Talk about Head Lice.* New York: Rosen Publishing
    Group, 1999.

Hartley, Karen, Chris Macro, and Philip Taylor. *Head Louse.* Chicago:
    Heinemann Library, 2000.

Royston, Angela. *Clean and Healthy.* Chicago: Heinemann Library, 1999.